Original Sin

Michael Foldes

Červená Barva Press
Somerville, MA

Červená Barva Press
P.O. Box 440357
Somerville, MA 02144-3222

www.cervenabarvapress.com

Bookstore: www.thelostbookshelf.com

Cover Art: Christopher Panzner

Cover Design: William J. Kelle

Production: Jonathan Penton

ISBN: 978-1-950063-73-4

Contents

*Dedicated to The WE ARE YOU PROJECT,
and the many friends there who give life to the arts.*

Original Sin

original sin

Part 1:

original sin

ah, to be old and able
to appreciate youthful
indiscretion, those
artful moments of
excitement and delivery
from the future
and the past, while
having a blast.

those mountains
of conformance
exploding into bits
of memories lost
in the instants
it took to rip them
rock from mound.

on a simple whim,
the driving force
behind invention
and consequence,
the original sin
clad in agnostic garb,
for whomever delights
in putting them on.

original sin

Part 2:

that was then
apologies to vb

the transparencies had been expected,
images of another time when we were
young, naked and unafraid.

not the kind of photographs
you want to share with strangers.
or your children.

pulled from the slide sheets,
they sat collected in a bag
until the decision was made.

the ash of their cremation
settled on newfallen snow.
the smoke was intoxicating.

and then i was alone again.

I Made Our Bed This Morning

I made our bed this morning.
Put on the yellow sheets to match
the rare sun shining through open blinds.
I don't think I've seen the sun like this,
or a clear blue sky, in weeks.

I only slept on your side of the bed once,
shortly after you left, to see if I could
still smell you there. What it felt like.
After that, I tried once, but it was as though
I were trespassing, using something not mine.

I've washed the sheets many times since.
I feel your presence occasionally, but
don't sense your smell. The smell, I miss.
The movement. And the touch.

It's been some time, now. When will you
be coming back? The depression on my side
of the bed is getting deeper, while
your side remains above it, a low-rise mesa.

While the depression on my side deepens
I wonder, is this to become my grave?

The outline of my body on the sheet
in the morning, and the deepening divide.
I made our bed this morning
and this is what came to mind.

carpet of words

i am rolling out the carpet of words.

in times like these temperatures rise
with the signature pose of youth gone mad
with love, enraptured, but not insensible,
accepting, accepting, accepting.

welcome to that juvenile world.

i am rolling out the red carpet of words.

the alphabet wrapped in wool, woven
into song, presents itself, cloaked, hooded,
yet visible to prince and peasant alike.

a gathering storm, a breaking sun,
rains quenching the garden's thirst,
readying roots for what's to come.

i roll out a crimson carpet of unintelligible words,
listen carefully to fringed and knotted ends
where watery winds pepper anxious ears.

walk on me, rehearse the voice, but
do not gut the warp and woof or risk
unraveling hopes entwined therein,
that cache of dreams hard brought to light
for those who read to find delight
in torrid tales of blossoming love.

Uma-Mahesvara

I have received this piece from others
where it settled in a Denver museum.
I hope you will rejoice in it with me
as I covet what is not mine before
it is returned to its rightful home,
a niche chiseled into the facade
of a stone wall, cemented onto a sill
in defense of culture and history.

We buried our treasure above ground
and shared it with the world
until one day a visitor recognized
what had long been missing,
and sought to ameliorate
the pain of Nepal's missing limb
by asking for its release
from its architectural tomb.

Wander halls anywhere and see
what is not yours or theirs,
where silence is weaponized
against return of what came
from somewhere else
by chance and circumstance.
Perhaps there was a time
that justified us to protect
these icons from war or strife,
perhaps they were acquired
by outright thievery,
or purchased in ignorance
devoid of suspected origins.

But once rediscovered in the silt
of civilization's manicured troves,
restoration became inevitable.
The Courts of Accountability
must dutifully find for return
of plunder to rightful heirs,
and heal their broken homes
with joyful reunion.

TWICE A VIRGIN
Sex & death in the time of Covid

dissociation

middle of the afternoon.
trapped at work.
can't reach out;
can't reach in.
congress muddles along.
covid inhibits reunion.
i understand why some people
run to the frig.
middle of the afternoon.
another espresso pot
gurgles on the stove
where i seek inspiration.
another banana won't do.
a cherry tomato, perhaps.
can't reach in.
trapped at work.
i'd write you a letter
but i've done that before
and the answer it seems
was lost somewhere.
what kind of fool
permits himself to walk
when standing still
gets him to the same place?
it is the middle of the afternoon,
I am trapped at work
tending the fields to see
what's trending.
down along argonne,
by the river, a deer
with its head blown off
thinks about voting.
I'd write you a longer letter
but my heart's run dry.

this is our tomorrow
january 21, 2021

the morning after,
no headache, no faltering,
no weakness,
no mild incantations
to protect one's self
from sleep into the day.
the sun may not be shining
but there is light passing through
the clouds and we can see,
at last, a life that beckons,
not threatens, to pull us
into its open arms.
this is our tomorrow,
the one we voted for,
the one we begged for,
the one we prayed for,
the one we received
by the powers of gods,
women, and men.
this is our day,
our tomorrow and
tomorrow's tomorrow,
animated by ideals,
shaped by imagination,
delivered on rivers
of blood, and hope
that it will not become simply
another cautionary tale.

tale for an afterlife

in memory of emerson burkhart

> *NOTE: Emerson Burkhart was a regionally known artist who lived*
> *in Columbus, Ohio. His work is included in numerous collections,*
> *including the Columbus Museum of Art.*

and when he died they asked
fuck, didn't he throw anything away?

and when he died they went through
his stuff and there was a shitload of it.

and when he died there wasn't anyone alive
who knew him well enough to sift the sands.

and when he died many came to know him
in ways he could only have imagined...

and when he died the brass box on a library shelf
with his wife's ashes became a doper's ashtray.

and when he died those parts of him of value,
dubious and otherwise, went round the world.

thus the paintings on our shadowy walls,
the bones of an afghan buried in a back yard

and other tales to be retold in an afterlife.

THE SEDITION EDITIONS

So here we all are, in our own, personalized bunkers.
The wall of fame around the Capitol has been breached.
The wall along the southern border got its last visit.
Now an army with physical presence stands watch
to see an invisible, secular, immutable rule is preserved.

The sedition editions of news papers and news broadcasts
echo loudly, as the put-upon take stock, admit fear, while
sycophants continue parroting lies, fabricated events,
and struggle to find reasons to believe the unfounded,
too weak to admit defeat, to see themselves as others do.

History screams "We are not a peaceful nation,"
Wars within, wars without, assassinations, genocide...
So much fades into history and seems lost,
when another face of calumny arrives to remind us,
given a chance, we are no different from the rest.

The barbarians, it seems, are always at the gate,
waiting, preparing for the time the civil tides ebb
and they can satisfy their coprophagic appetites
on what they believe to be the dead or dying
bodies of Liberty, Democracy and Truth.

So here we all are, many of us driven underground
by weak-minded, ill-intentioned individuals led by
absurdity itself onto the minefields of what
another man imagined would put him safely
in the ranks of Nero, Caligula, Hitler...

Now that it's time to come out of hiding
and show gratitude a little old lady had
the gumption and fortitude to declare
not only is "enough enough," but to put
accountability on trial, and not just a man.

Should another charlatan try again to stack the deck,
precedent will grease the wheels of justice
so ignominious powers wither and die like
hatred and lies in gardens of truth and dignity.
As for the followers? Some people just won't learn.

wars we wage with words

i am not a student of verse
but feel addicted to it, and
from an early age. not
the nursery rhymes, but
those were, at the time,
all right to listen to, too.
but later on, when writing
itself took hold, as if
i were living alone and
talking to myself, as
i am prone to do today.
my classes in poetics
were dappling sun
on magical thickets
in forlorn landscapes,
shedding just enough light
to nourish fascination with,
if not a full grasp of,
poetry. thus, i write
and still, occasionally,
turn to books and sites
for lessons never learned
– or simply forgotten –
to find the rules I bend
and remind myself
the games we play,
the wars we wage,
the words we engage
must be of our own.
that only one letter more
would make them swords.

night-crawlers

all the clever has gone out of me.
you can tell when someone has had enough.
their dedication to discovery dissolves.
footsteps in the morning snow
were there before you arrived.
someone always has to be first.
a neighbor shoveling his walk says,
"i see you walking.
it's a good time to walk."
happy new year, i reply.
"happy new year," he answers,
the sun will be up, soon.
i am in no hurry to bend and lift.
the sun will take care of that.
i do not see the world today
the way i saw the world yesterday.
closing my eyes, the visions
do not collect adjectives and adverbs
as i would like. they are stark,
without much life. that's the depth
of winter, for you. all black and white
where are the colors others see?
a collective failure on my part?
a junkyard piled high with rusting cars;
an oil barrel and a rat.
the neighborhood park with swings,
pavilion, basketball court.
when was the last time
you courted? or were?
do you remember turning
the moss-covered dirt
by the creek by the spring
to dig up night-crawlers?
who is going to dig us out?

the watching device
january 7, 2021

what i saw yesterday,
what we all saw yesterday,
was enough to make me sick.
not sure what you may have felt,
and those of you who did not see,
or were not alive to see
should read this 100 years from now,
might have felt similarly
had you been there,
on site, or in front of your
watching device,
whatever that watching device
may have been.
today the lackeys who stayed on
for the sense of entitlement
they enjoyed are jumping ship.
the ship is not going down,
but the captain is.
and so should they,
having been given trust
they did not deserve
and responsibility
they failed to provide.
as someone said on my
watching device,
"another day that will live
in infamy..."
what we saw yesterday
is, indeed, one for the books,
an attempt on the life
and liberty of a nation
dazed and confused
by the words of a crazed autocrat

whose misguided efforts
to dismantle the democracy
and join the ranks of dictators
speak for themselves.
a plague upon his house.
may he never rest in peace.

On Dreams:
No Reservations Needed

What are dreams, but reflections of ourselves?
The last music you hear echoes
through the night, stays until erased
by what you hear in the morning.
That essential element, bivouaced
in soft tissue called the brain,
protected in its shell of bone,
has the rest of you to thank,
like a humble performer
sharing the stage with other
members of the orchestra.

It's no accident we are here,
struggling together, striving
to make our separate ways
through this brittle biosphere.
Why now remember Persephone?
Was she once my lover? Why now
explore changes bodies go through
to metamorphose from infant to geriatric?
Why now furtive glances
into this future of the past,
this crystal common to us all?
The heart, the brain, lungs, liver –
Why make one more
important than another
when it's the skin
that holds it all together?
That soft shell angels and gods
peel away to harvest
our stored realities,
our shared experience.

The vanished, leaving art, artistry,
a few drawn characters, behind,
curious remnants occasionally
surfacing like bones of uncles
from the muck of riverbanks,
adding dimension to the puzzle.
We travelers hit upon a cornucopia
that illuminates the darkness
when we are without a sun,
that feeds us round the clock,
no reservations needed,
but blessed to have had one.

What are dreams, but reflections
of ourselves? The last music
you heard echoing until buried
in the midden of days.

the meth of sisyphus

i wrote an email to a friend in france
on presidents' day explaining that
due to the holiday i was able to work
at my own speed. it came to mind
that could be almost anything,
an old billy idol tune, or abrasive,
as someone about to lose his last tooth
who won't get out of your face.
time was a little crystal on the gums
was all one needed to get through
the night. and later, through the day.
there's godspeed, and then there's meth.
who would hold up the heavens
with a gun when there's chemistry
to help him out? uncanny what comes
to mind when one's mind recreates
that atmosphere of clarity and distortion
that follows the ingestion
of certain pharmaceuticals
some come to rely on for survival
and in which others find redemption.
we used to talk about a natural high
but from the time we drink
our mother's milk until the day we die
there is no other. just a matter
of natural selection which to ingest
inhale, imbibe. johnny, boy, eat
what's on the table. finish your plate.
there are starving people in the world.
what bullshit are we feeding them.
it's presidents' day and we are working
at our own speed, some with, others without.

gravity

gravity.
of the crease.
of the moment.
with the one hand
i reach out,
with the other i
i want to pray,
but praying is not
something
i do
with one hand
or two.
i seed my ground,
my future,
with hope.
prayer
is for believers.
make me
a believer
so i can both
hope and pray.
when gravity
takes me where
all things go,
pray
what's there
will make me
the believer
you said
i would become.

An Old Man Obsesses

I used to obsess about sex.
Now I obsess about death.
Necromancy? Dancing
in the dark? The passion
of dreams, or the dreams
of passion? Not much left
to obsess about, really.
Sex was then. This is now.
Not unusual. Inevitable.

The quandary of youth,
sex – how to have it
and make it work.
Not disappoint, or be
disappointed. Now
a virgin at another door,
Every movement, foreplay.
Trying again to make it last.
Not disappoint.
Or be disappointed.

footballer

i am not interested in winning arguments
because i am not interested in having arguments.
we have been pushing for decades
but the mountain has not moved.
the rivers have not stopped flowing to the sea
and the sea still rolls onto shore, dropping
kelp and shells that will survive on shelves
long after echoes of the screams subside,
long after photos of the scenes fade to white.
I am not interested in having arguments,
but i do enjoy a good football game now and then.

kickstarter

got an email today
from kickstarter, subject:
projects we love – fornication.
lost interest when
i read it again, realized
it said fortification.

The Momentum

I like to watch movies
with lots of intrigue —
lots of violence — the movies
that warn "The following
is for mature audiences.
Contains gore, nudity, profanity,
smoking..."
It's the smoking that really gets me.
Most of the time no one smokes, but
it's easier for the censors to put that in
as part of the blanket than view
each and every film.

When someone does smoke,
I often wonder if it's the brand
the script writer smokes.
Or if it's the brand I smoked
back in the day, when a line or two,
a needle, a cactus bud, a sugar cube
or candy heart were as readily
available as smokes, though
not over-the-counter
as the herb is today.
I joked with friends my body
was my test tube – a lab to see
what worked, what really worked,
to take me to that other place.
And what didn't. When I got sick,
I moved on, and away ... the surprise
when one of my old pals passed
was not what it should have been.
A reaction more like, "Must have been
some really bad shit." The cynic
never far behind.

If you survived it all —
until the scene was over,
when the thrill was gone,
when you thought you'd
done it all but die,
there was life to consider.
And getting on with it.
The marvelous normal things
people do when they desire
to grow old and die peacefully.
No lightning. No thunder.

A guy I knew used to joke he wanted
to go out at 75, shot in the back
by a jealous husband. Actually
he was shot in the stomach
at 35 and never walked again.

I tried a few times to put out
my own lights. The last effort
ended up not such a great idea.
Kind of boring, really, a long
couple of nights in and out
of bed to piss, the rest of the time
lying in the dirt in a dark field
of dried flowers wondering when
the scenery was going to change.
It never did. A distant voice
inquiring, "Is this what you really want?"
Death gave me momentum to cruise
the known and unknown universe.
I was one of the lucky ones.

talk at the end of days

so, you say you are dying and take advantage
of your situation to get some things off your chest
without fear of too much blowback,
figuring those who are the targets
of your longstanding preferences
to take offense at what were not meant
to be offensive will bow and bend
to your single-minded way of seeing.

is it rather harsh of me to ignore
your poorly disguised plea to reconnect
and come back at you with remembrances
that will be difficult to sleep with
when you need rest, but now that you
have brought things up that make it hard
for me to sleep as well, i thought i'd share.
we seem to remember things differently,
or store them in such a way as to fit them
into the various cubbies in our brains.

where you have no problem sharing
what you perceived as slights and insults,
that were taken unkindly and let to simmer
for years in the pot with bile, i am ashamed.
not ashamed for what i may have said
or done, but that i do not remember
verbatim what maligned either of us.
you bringing all that up again does
remind me, though, of your divisiveness
and why i did not reach out.

now that our cards are on the table
and we are down to the last few plays,
better the truth resonates,
reminders and rejoinders
too far removed to fit properly
or stop the bleeding
in the jagged puzzle we have made.

empty cups

good morning.
i love you.
the golden past,
the afghan
and the staircase
you don't remember.

so long since i've heard
those words, i love you.
i say them to myself
because you won't.
or can't.

when we see each other
again will there be light,
or fire? will there be
cloud cover and wind?
just what to expect?

the causeway from the mainland
to the island is under water.
what will be exposed
when the water recedes?

harmony in the microwave
when the espresso reheats
to a right temperature.
are we to be left with empty cups,
or a satisfying return to action.

war is so fucked

Note: "This week marks the 50-year anniversary of Larry Burrows's death.
On February 10th, 1971, the helicopter in which he was traveling to photograph the invasion of Laos was shot down, killing all on board." I wrote this poem after reading an article in L'Oeil de la Photographie and seeing some of what he photographed before he died. Are the people of Vietnam better off today than then? Debatable, of course, but they're not dying "from the bombs and the guns."

war is so fucked
don't know how else
to say it.
can't understand why
some revel in it.
the guts and glory?
war is so fucked
but at the end
of the day
what else is there
when the fires
are burning
and there's no other way
to put them out.

escape from reading gaol
mural attributed to banksy, march 2021

the artist scales a wall to paint a mural.
the artist scales a wall to make a point.
the artist makes a point by scaling
the wall that held oscar wilde close,
the wall that birthed the "ballad of reading gaol."
is the picture on the wall worth a thousand words,
or more? far more than a thousand have been written
in the few days since the artist scaled the wall.
even i am adding to the mass, compounding
what appears to be a simple plan to escape
the monotony of containment in the time of covid.
the artist scales a wall to paint a mural,
leaves the escapee hanging on the tale,
caught by imagination, captured by the eye.

Voices

I am hearing voices.
I turn off the television.
The voices persist.
There is no one in the street outside
where the rain is turning to snow.
There is enough snow on the ground
that people could easily be seen.
Streetlights cast light on the snow
where there are no footprints,
no tracks of tires, boots, deer, rabbits,
squirrels, cats. An empty scene
replete with silence.

This is not the first time.
Usually the voices are unclear,
as if there were a mingling crowd
in a foreign film, a shot taken
from afar, soundtrack up close.
More than once
they've gotten close, too close,
close enough to say, "Go on, do it."
And I did. If pills were something
other than what they were
I might have slept a lifetime.
Tonight the crowd outside
will dissipate. I will extinguish
the lamp on the nightstand
beside the bed where I read
someone else's poetry.
Are they writing in tongues?
Why so much confusion?

Wireless signals all around.
Is that what I hear? What I see?
Why, outside, is no one there?
This race against time. They
ask me to join them.
I reply, "I tried and was refused,"
tell them I am making my home here now,
that one day when I am ready and
another voice comes to me I may
come along, but for now,
once was enough.

never grow up

i wish i never grew up
i mean, not from childhood,
but from the 20s, when
life is at its highest.
before the drugs
and alcohol, sex and
long nights, and other
commitments extracted
their undeniable tolls.
i wish i never grew up
from the days a night
in bed with a crowd
of strangers who also
had not grown up,
was what one sought
with high-pitched fever.
a knot of bodies in a story
we'd read about and
then were words in print.
looking back now with
scant aplomb, i wish
i had never grown up
to be what i've become,
a shrinking cabinet
of shredded memories,
confetti for a funeral.
i do wonder, though, how
i moved this far away
from that, and why
there is no way to reach
across and take it back
when at times it feels so near.
where a photograph
becomes the first frame
in a lifelong film captured
then replayed in fading color.

idle portrait

where did we begin?
with what line?
what mark?
what idea?
what part of the face?
what part of the mouth?
was it a line,
an idea, or a challenge?
where do we go
          from here?
where is the ladder?
where are the stars?

Acknowledgements

For most of us, poetry will never put food on the table. For the rest, it's often enough to just keep writing. When fortune shines, friendships are formed that open doors to the sharing and exchange of ideas, thoughts and emotions that provide food for the soul. It was my good fortune a few years ago to discover the Art of Christopher Panzner, whose virtual acquaintance metamorphosed into a real friendship yielding tangible results, including two ekphrastic collaborations, and the cover of this chapbook. I still work to put food on the table, but Chris's appreciation and understanding of my words have helped keep me writing – and sane – throughout the recent period of isolation.

Thanks also to Gloria Mindock, who cared enough to bring this book to light; to Jose Rodeiro, Paul Sohar, Nick Buglaj, Christie Devereux, Alan Britt, Joe Weil, Steve Poleskie and so many others. Finally, *et con gravitas*, you, dear reader, whose time is always of the essence.

Thank You for Reading.

About the Author

Michael Foldes (b 1946) is an American poet, publisher, author and businessman. Born in Baltimore, MD, he grew up in Endwell, New York, later graduating from The Ohio State University in anthropology. In 2004, Foldes founded Ragazine.cc, a free, global, online magazine of art, information and entertainment. The bi-monthly zine ceased publication in December 2019. Partial archives remain online at www.ragazine.cc.

Foldes's publications and projects include the anthologies "Stopped Dead: The End of Poetry," "In an Early Hour," and "Sand and Snow"; *Sleeping Dogs: A true story of the Lindbergh baby kidnapping*" (Split Oak Press, Ithaca, NY, 2012), and *Sandy: Chronicles of a Superstorm* in collaboration with artist Christie Devereaux. In 2017, he completed *Fashions & Passions*" a series of ekphrastic poems in collaboration with artist Christopher Panzner. Panzner and Foldes recently completed a second collection titled "End Game," 75 poems with images created by Panzner in response to the poems. His poetry collection *Some Stuff* is available as a Kindle edition on Amazon.

Foldes's articles, editorials, poems, reviews, interviews and stories have appeared in publications worldwide, some in translation in Romanian, Hungarian, Japanese, French and Spanish. Publishing credits include *l'Oeil de la Photographie, Where is the Jazz Festival, Mobius, Southern Literary Review, the Village Voice, High Times, The Seventh Quarry, Paterson Literary Review, CLH/Romania, We Are You Poetry* anthology, *From the Finger Lakes, Folazil* (France), and *Rosebud*, among others. An interview with Foldes by Carol Smallwood appeared in the *Scarlet Leaf Review*, and in *Wilderness House Literary Review*.

His jobs have included lifeguard, grocery store bagger, potato peeler, construction worker, magazine editor, newspaper editor, social worker, electronic component sales rep, and medical video products sales engineer. One of his favorite gigs was bartending at the National Poetry Society in Earl's Court Square, London, where the Guinness was warm and the patrons amazing.

He and his wife have three children and two grandchildren. They live in New York's Southern Tier a few hundred yards from the Susquehanna River.

www.ingramcontent.com/pod-product-compliance
Lightning Source LLC
LaVergne TN
LVHW041205080426
835511LV00006B/742